# FAMILIES

## by
## Meredith Tax

## Illustrated by Marylin Hafner

*An Atlantic Monthly Press Book*

Little, Brown and Company
BOSTON        TORONTO

FIRST EDITION

*Library of Congress Cataloging in Publication Data*

Tax, Meredith.
    Families.

    "An Atlantic Monthly Press Book."
    SUMMARY: Describes different kinds of families.
    1. Family — United States — Juvenile literature.
[1. Family] I. Hafner, Marylin. II. Title.
HQ536.T39        306.8        80-21316
ISBN 0-316-83240-5

ATLANTIC-LITTLE, BROWN BOOKS
ARE PUBLISHED BY
LITTLE, BROWN AND COMPANY
IN ASSOCIATION WITH
THE ATLANTIC MONTHLY PRESS

BP

*Published simultaneously in Canada*
*by Little, Brown & Company (Canada) Limited*

PRINTED IN THE UNITED STATES OF AMERICA

To Corey and her friends at P.S. 75
— M. T.

For Nanny and Dave, family, too.
— M. H.

62306

My name is Angie. I am six. Here is everything I know about families.

Families are who you live with and who you love. I live with my mother most of the time and with my father on vacations. I also have two grandmas and one grandpa and some aunts and uncles and cousins. They are all in my family, but I don't live with them.

My mother and I live in a big building in New York. We have a laundry in the basement. I help do the wash: I carry the soap and put the money in the slot and fold the dry clothes. Then my mother says, "Thank you, partner," and kisses my nose.

My father lives in Boston with my stepmother, Alice. They have a little baby named Mickey. He's my half brother. We have the same father but not the same mother so he's only a half, but he's just as good as a whole.

I help burp him after he has his bottle. The burp sounds as loud as a firecracker and makes me laugh. Then Mickey smiles too. My father says it's because his stomach feels better, but I think it's because he's glad I'm there.

This is a lion's family: one father, one mother, and three cubs. They all live together in a cage at the zoo. My friend George also lives with one father, one mother, and two brothers — but not in a cage.

His big brother, Gus, is nine. Sometimes he lets us play baseball with him, but we never get to bat. I'm the catcher. George says that when his baby brother can walk he'll let him be the catcher, then I can pitch and George will be the batter. I say we should all share.

This is my friend Marisel from school. She has a big family. She lives with her mother, her Aunt Rosa, her grandma and grandpa, her brothers, Carlos and Hector, and her baby sister, Marianna. Her father and another grandma live in Puerto Rico. Marisel's Aunt Rosa works in a dress factory. She is very good at making clothes, and made Marisel a pink party dress for her birthday.

When I went to Marisel's party, her Aunt Rosa looked at the label in my dress and started to laugh. She said she made my dress too, when she was at work! I said, "It's a good thing you did or I wouldn't have anything to wear."

Marisel taught me to say hello in Spanish.

This is my cousin Louie. He's adopted. That means he didn't come from my Aunt Julie's belly, but they got him someplace else. They get to keep him forever, though. Louie is very tough. He broke his arm falling out of a tree and only cried a little. Aunt Julie says she loves every bone in his body and hopes he doesn't break them all before he's ten.

15

These are ants. They live in a glass box in my school. There is only one mother ant, the queen, but lots of fathers and hundreds and hundreds of tiny babies. You can hardly see them, they're so small. When I was little I used to step on ants, but now I don't because their families might be sad.

Frederick Douglas has two beds! One is at his mother's and the
other downstairs at his grandma's. He stays downstairs during the week
because his mother works nights in a bakery and his grandma brings
him to school in the morning.

On weekends he stays with his mom, and she takes him to the playground and brings a big bag of donuts from her job and gives them to all the kids. I like Frederick Douglas's mother.

This is my mom's friend Emma. She lives with Arthur. They have no kids but they like them to visit. They have a collection of sixteen paperweights with snow falling inside, and they let me play with them. I try to make them all snow at once.

Here is a family of chickens. They live together in a chicken coop.
There are lots of mother hens but only one father for all these baby
chicks. He's a rooster.

Willie lives with his father. He knows how to sew on Willie's buttons when they come off, and he makes him pancakes and bacon every Sunday morning. He invited our whole class on Willie's birthday — twenty-five kids! My mother said, "You've got to be kidding," but

he said, "You're only five once." There was a great big cake with super-heroes all over it because Willie wants to be a superhero when he grows up. All the other parents helped clean up after the party because it got a little messy.

Susie lives with her mother and her godmother. They took her to the roller disco and she won a prize for the best skater under twelve. The prize was a pin like a silver roller skate. When I asked Susie where her father lives, she said she doesn't have any father.

So George said he would be her father. Then Frederick Douglas said he wanted to be her father too, so we had to let them both do it. Susie was the baby and Willie was the brother and Marisel was the mother. I got to be the teacher. Kids can be like families too.

Some dogs have people for a family. They only live with their own mothers when they are babies; after that they move out and live with people. But when they see other dogs in the street, they are very interested. A woman in our building has four dogs, but I don't think they are brothers because they look so different.

Sometimes I wish my parents both lived in one house like George's, or at least in the same city. But he wants to be like me. He asked his mom when she was going to get a divorce because he wants to fly to Boston all by himself. "It's not fair," he told me. So I said he could come with me if he lets me ride his bike whenever I want.

There are lots of different kinds of families. Some are big and some are small. Some are animals and some are people. Some live in one house and some live in two or three.

The main thing isn't where they live or how big they are —

it's how much they love each other.